Anglo-S Days

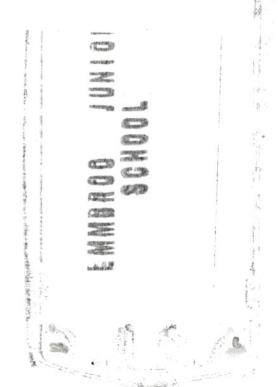

Contents

Start your day	2
Collect and mend	6
Gathering food	10
Fun and games	18
Feast and dance	20
An Anglo-Saxon day	30

Written by Lindsay Galvin
Illustrated by Mike Phillips

Collins

Start your day

It is daybreak in this typical Anglo-Saxon village. The cock crows and the neighbours are pottering around.

That means you need to wake up straightaway.
You leap up and throw off your animal skin covers.

It's cramped in the shared room of your wooden hut.

Comb your hair. Change into strong, windproof clothing and waterproof shoes, as most Anglo-Saxon work is outside.

5

Collect and mend

It is time for your usual chores. Your first mission is to go to the forest with your father to collect water and sticks.

Wood is essential for the fires that provide heat and cook the food.

Back at the village, some men are mending the reeds and straw on the thatched roofs.

Your sister is busy weaving sheep's wool on the loom to make cloth. Mothers and daughters work together. There's no school here – your mum and dad teach you everything you know.

Gathering food

The Anglo-Saxon village keeps animals for food. Your next task is to go to the chicken pen to collect eggs.

Your sister has trotted past the beehives and over the bridge to the sheep field. Is she thinking that sheep lay eggs?

Be cautious! Don't go too close to the hives ...
That buzzing is a bad sign.

The bees are in an atrocious mood! Try to dodge them. Ouch!

Anglo-Saxons can't let a bee-sting stop them, even when it really hurts.

Back at the hut, the fire is going out. Grab the wood to feed the fire.

Why is your sister mixing sheep poo with an egg?

Of course! It's a special potion for the bee-sting. Rubbing it on your thumb is a bit smelly, but it seems to help a bit.

The villagers cheer when a hunter returns.

He caught a large fish to share at this evening's meal!

Fun and games

The other children are back from the fields, where they've been helping to harvest the barley. Your chores are done for now. It's time to play a board game!

Your sister is deep in concentration as she strings beads on leather to make a bracelet. Anglo-Saxons love jewellery. What a great design!

Feast and dance

Usually, Anglo-Saxons eat simple food like bread, cheese and eggs. But today is a special occasion! The villagers are gathering in the hall for a feast. This is the time they can socialise and share news.

The fish is cooked over the roaring fire. Delicious! You have a drink from your cow's horn cup.

A musician plays a drum, and a song starts up on the panpipes. Neighbours sing.

Your sister usually loves to dance but she is too tired from her day of chores. You know what to do!

Anglo-Saxon clothing

- linen tunic
- wool tunic
- leather belt
- pouch
- knife with deer antler handle
- leather shoes

bead and brass earrings

wool overdress

long linen underdress

Anglo-Saxon remedies
(Caution – may contain poo)

For a burn – burnt goat poo, wheat stalks and butter, heated over a fire and smeared onto the burn

For a sore throat – white dog poo (from a dog that has eaten bones) mixed with honey and painted on the neck

For earache – garlic and goose fat melted together and squeezed in the ear

Anglo-Saxon fun and games

board games

jewellery-making

28

music, singing and dancing

cloth dolls

storytelling

An Anglo-Saxon day

🐾 Review: After reading 🐾

Use your assessment from hearing the children read to choose any GPCs, words or tricky words that need additional practice.

Read 1: Decoding
- Turn to pages 2 and 3. Ask the children which word tells us that it is first thing in the morning. (**daybreak**) Which word tells us that you must get up immediately and not lie about in bed? (**straightaway**)
- Ask the children to read these words, breaking down the words into syllables if necessary.

  essential (*ess/en/tial*)   **musician** (*mu/si/cian*)
  atrocious (*a/tro/cious*)   **concentration** (*con/cen/tra/tion*)

- Turn to page 20. Point to **occasion**, allowing the children to sound and blend out loud. Repeat for **socialise**. Then encourage the children to read the page silently, blending in their heads, before reading the words aloud.

Read 2: Prosody
- Ask the children to read pages 12 and 13 as if they were a narrator in a play. Challenge them to use pauses and changes in tone to make the information sound as exciting as possible. For example:
  - On page 12, encourage them to pause at the ellipsis, to make the reader wait and see what happens next.
  - On page 13, discuss how to say **Ouch!** to show that the boy has been stung.
- Bonus content: Challenge the children to read pages 26 and 27 with appropriate expression. Discuss which words to emphasise to make the information sound both funny and disgusting.

Read 3: Comprehension
- Discuss what the children already know about Anglo-Saxons and how they lived. Would they like to live in an Anglo-Saxon village? Why?
- Turn to pages 20 and 21. Discuss whether the people in the village gathered to have fun very often. (e.g. *no, they only gathered for a feast day*) Ask: Why do you think this was? (e.g. *they were too busy with chores on most days*)
- Turn to pages 30 and 31. Challenge the children to explain what village life is like for the boy in the book. Encourage them to recall details, asking questions such as: When did he have to wake up? (*daybreak*) What music did they dance to at the feast? (e.g. *drum, panpipes and singing*)